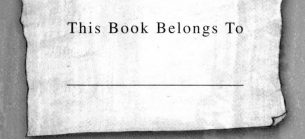

This Book Belongs To

_____

I ♥ BUGS

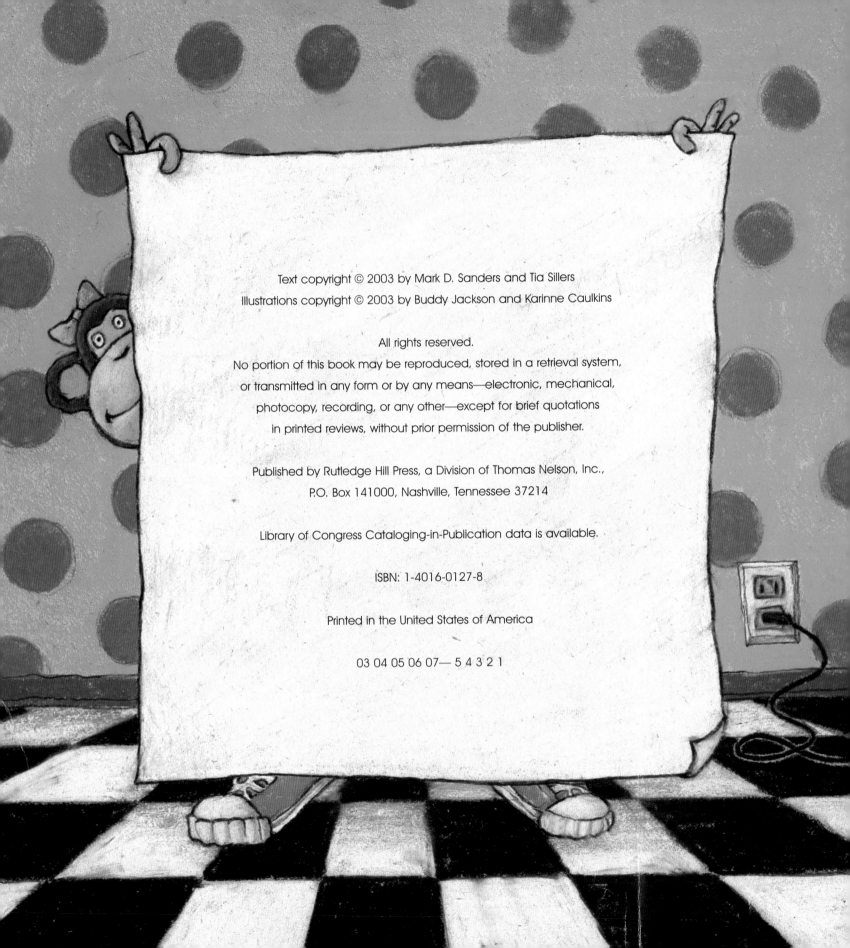

Published by Rutledge Hill Press, a Division of Thomas Nelson, Inc.,

P.O. Box 141000, Nashville, Tennessee 37214

Library of Congress Cataloging-in-Publication data is available.

ISBN: 1-4016-0127-8

Printed in the United States of America

03 04 05 06 07— 5 4 3 2 1

I HOPE YOU DANCE!

By Mark D. Sanders & Tia Sillers

Pictures by Buddy Jackson & Karinne Caulkins

Rutledge Hill Press® | Nashville, Tennessee

A DIVISION OF THOMAS NELSON, INC. | WWW.THOMASNELSON.COM

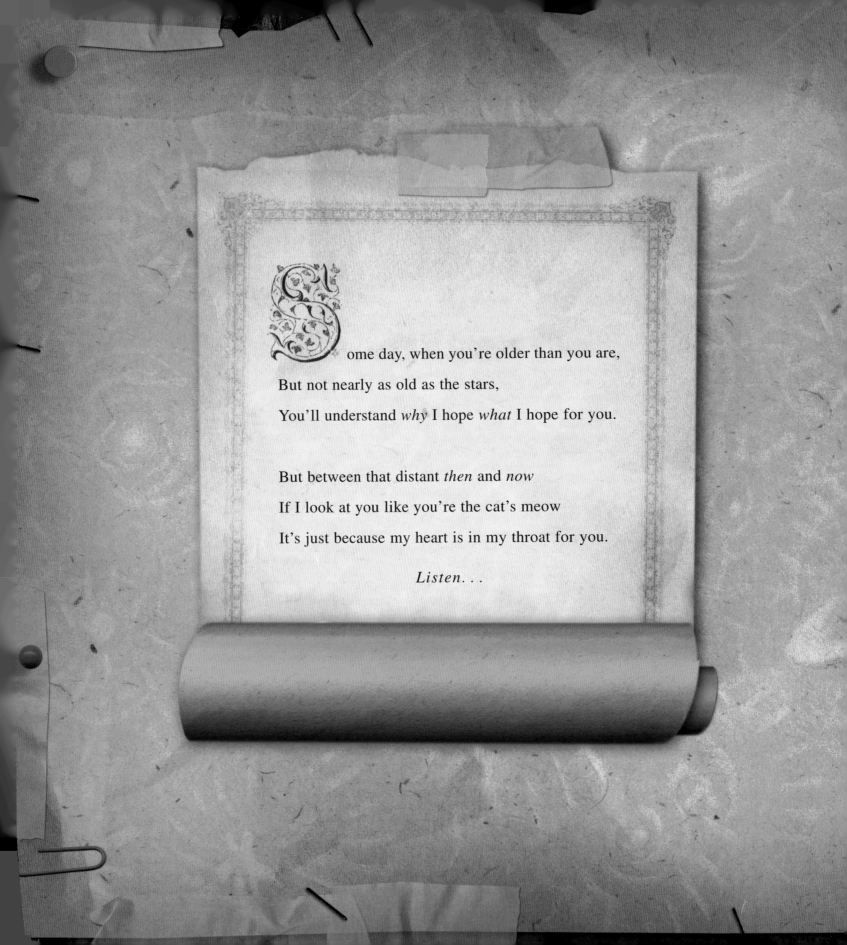

Some day, when you're older than you are,

But not nearly as old as the stars,

You'll understand *why* I hope *what* I hope for you.

But between that distant *then* and *now*

If I look at you like you're the cat's meow

It's just because my heart is in my throat for you.

Listen. . .

When your MAMA RAVES
and your DADDY RANTS,

or if by chance
it's the other way
around,

I hope
you're

NEVER EVER
LOST
AND ALWAYS
FOUND.

I HOPE YOU DANCE

Like a ballerina or a

CHIMPANZEENA

going by the name of TRINA, which, AFTER ALL, is a fitting name for some Simian* of

DANCING FAME!

sim·i·an: (sim-e-an) –*n.*

An ape, or one who apes about.

When it's pourin' rain and bangin' thunder,
I hope you NEVER misplace your
WONDERFUL
WONDER.
After all, those kangaroos down UNDER
aren't upside down, they're UPSIDE UP –
just like the orange juice in your CUP!
Just like your uncle in his PICK UP TRUCK!

It's gravity
that keeps us on the ground,
walking on our legs,
even though the world is ROUND,
kinda like
an EGG!

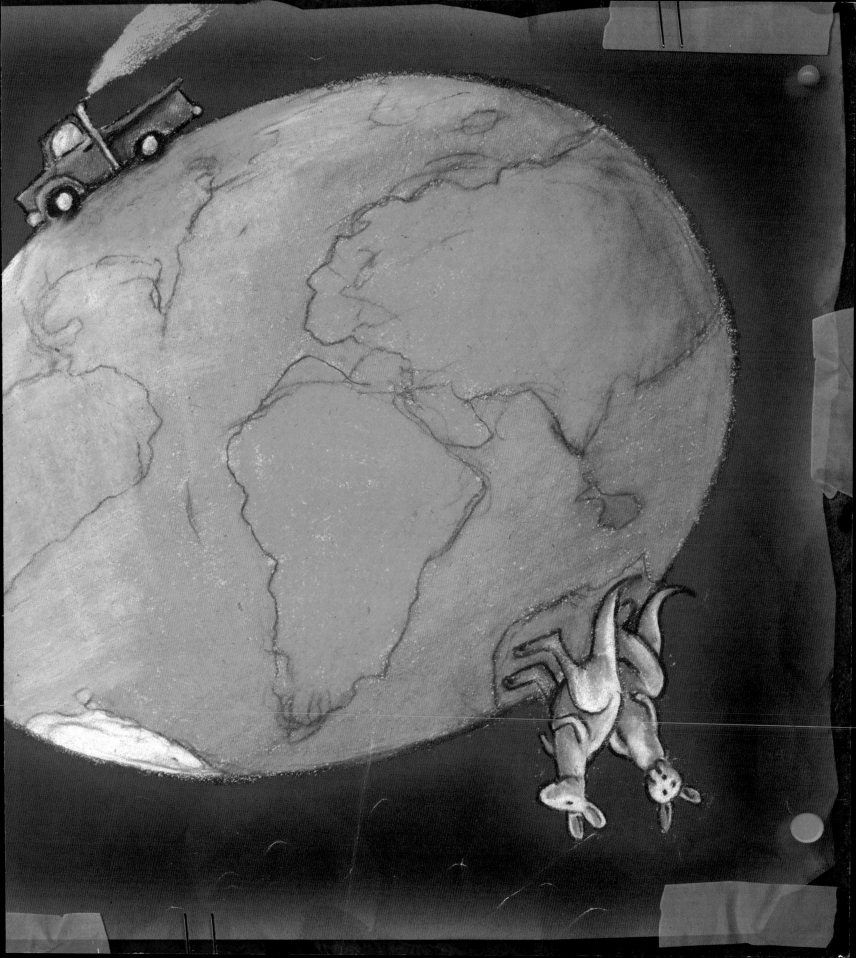

And which came first?
the EGG or the CHICKEN?!
If that won't make your gray matter THICKEN,
I don't know what WILL.
- AND STILL -

a million questions more
are just out side of
every DOOR

AND at the end of every MILE
AND under the dirty
LAUNDRY PILE.
YES, I Said
UNDER!

I hope you never misplace your

WONDERFUL WONDER!

I HOPE YOU DANCE!

AND if by chance your underpants
are inside out or outside in

I hope your GRIN GIGGLES
AND your GIGGLE GRINS...

AND you cackle with LAUGHTER 'cause, AFTER ALL,
the SUPER-EST thing about UNDERPANTS
is the way they RHYME WITH...

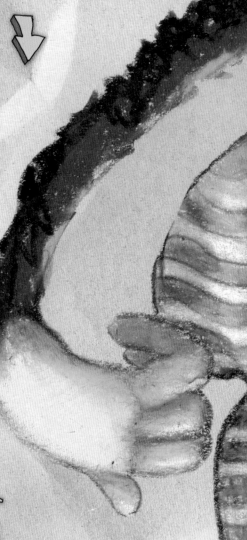

I HOPE YOU DANCE!

Don't lie in the tub and bubble bath SOAKA.
Get your SHIMMY on the floor and do the
ZYDECO POLKA!
Do the cotton-eyed Joe
and the HOKEY POKEY.
If you ain't got rhythm,
that's OKEY DOKEY.

Isn't that a mouthful?
Kinda makes your tongue PRICKLY.
Now try to say it five times QUICKLY!
QUICKLIER!
QUICKLIEST!
And once you feel you've
done your best...

I hope whenever one door CLOSES,
you and Trina follow your NOSES.
Never lose sight of what you're searchin' FOR—
turn left, then right, then left once MORE
until you find another open DOOR.
HOCUS! POCUS! ☺ SESAME SEEDS!
Those OPEN doors are the doors you NEED!
Some doors CREAK.
Some doors are SCARY.
Believe it or not, some doors are
HAIRY.
But never all that very
(scary or hairy).

And speaking of doors, let's shut that TOPIC.
How 'bout we Embark on a trip to the TROPICS?
we'll eat tapioca as in PUDDING or PIE.
We can HULA and LIMBO with the WATUSI TRIBE.
Those WATUSI are swell; those WATUSI are SWEET;

those Watusi would NEVER throw

MUD AT YOUR FEET.

WELCOME TO
WATUSI
CITY
HOME OF THE SWELL
LAND OF THE SWEET
LIMBO WORLD CHAMPS

EXPRESS

And speaking of MUD (yet another fine pie),
I hope no one EVER throws mud in your EYE.
But oh if they DO, if at first you BOO-HOO,
—that's all right— If at second you LAUGH,
Then go take a BATH! Go scrub in the Shower,
rub-a-dub in the RAIN, till all of that MUD
waltzes down the DRAIN.
And now that you're CLEAN, it's the
Perfect chance for ME to mention . . .

I hope you rock like a rocker
and roll like a roller
and PAINT like a roller...or a brush.
I hope you RUSH
out onto The living room floor
and say, "TURN IT UP, MAMA!
TURN IT UP
MORE!"

and I lose my hair and I wear a WIG.
Oh! I hope it doesn't come to that.
But if it does, I have to say
I hope we can laugh at my bad toupee.

Who needs hair anyway?
If you don't like my wig,
rest assured you MAY
polish my head until it shines
like a BOWLING BALL
or A PORCUPINE
(without the Needles, needless to SAY).

Needless to say we're near the last pagina,*
which is Spanish for page and
rhymes with TRINA.
Oh, and TRINA,
because she's a chimpanzee,
sorta likes to eat ANTS
sorta likes to eat FLEAS!

Yipes! I hope YOU DON'T
and I hope YOU WON'T
develop a taste for fleas and ants —
BUT there's one thing Trina does

* say it like pa-HEE-na

that I HOPE YOU DO...

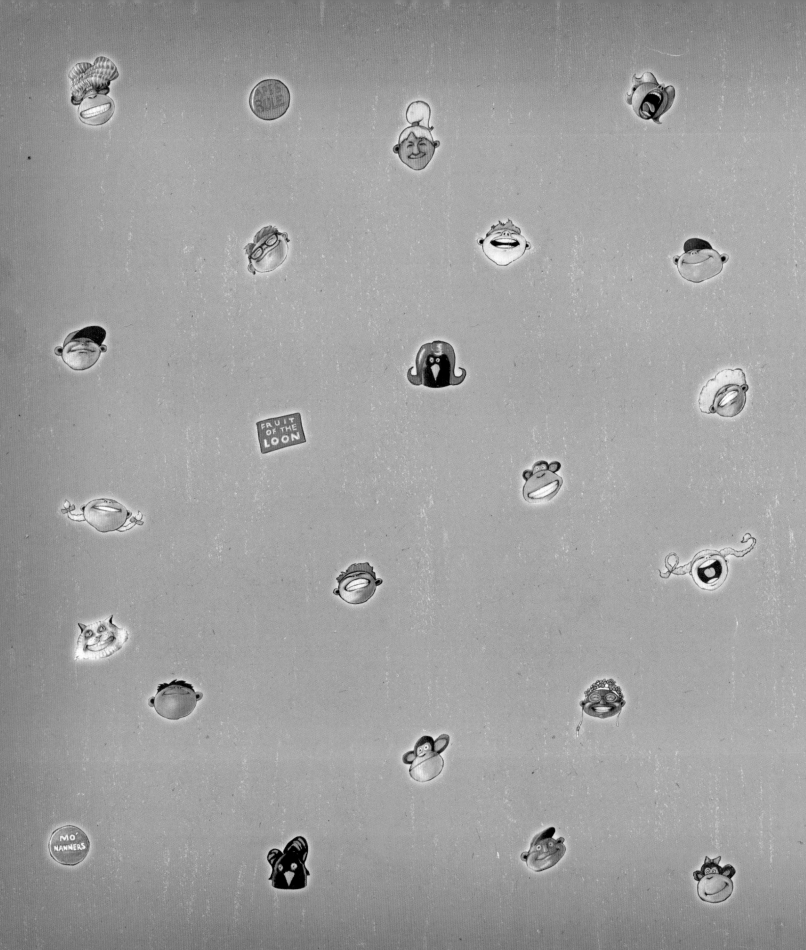